People at Work

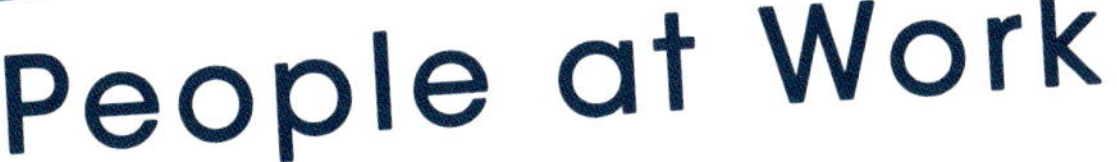

Working at an Airport

by Connor Stratton

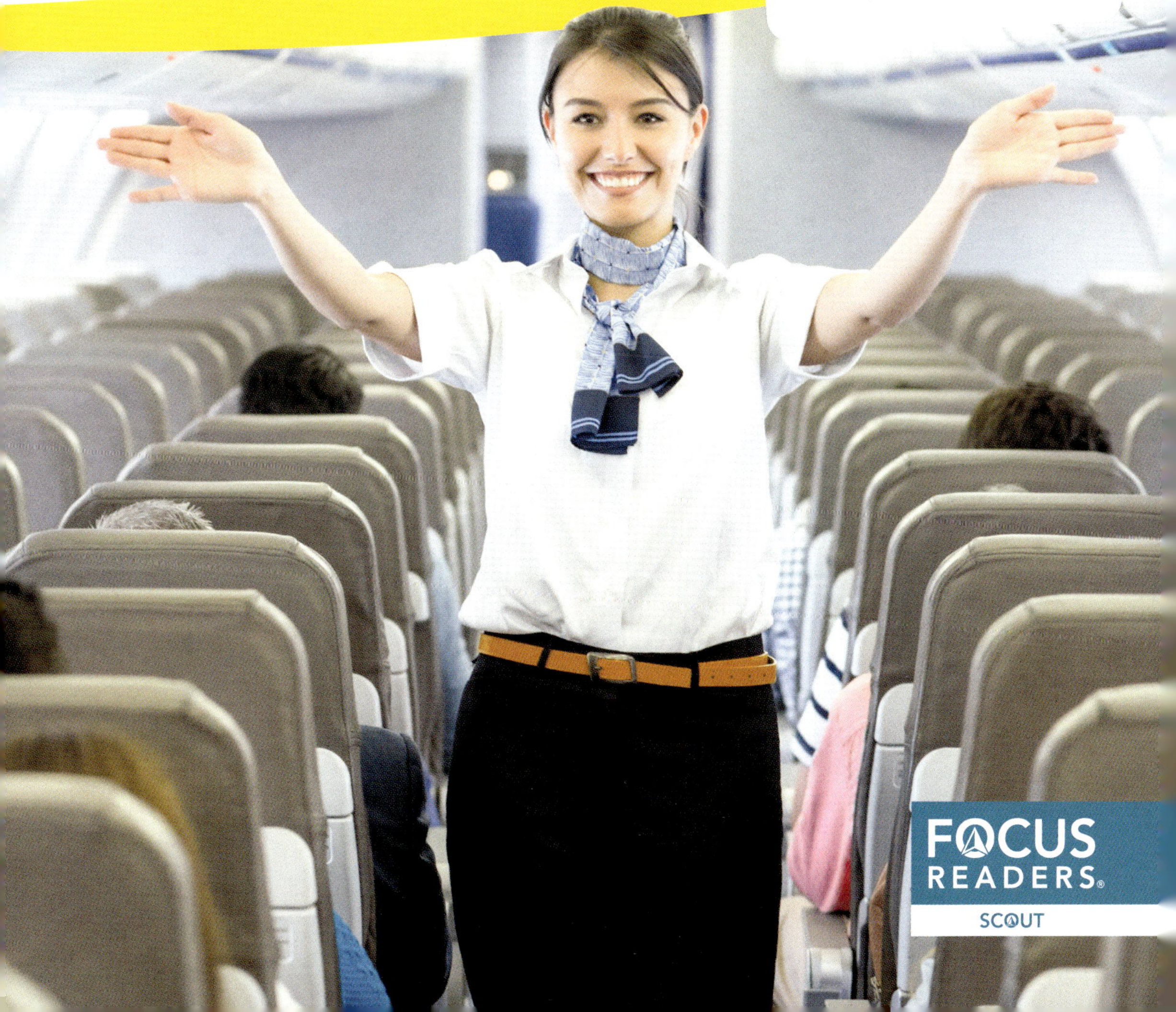

FOCUS READERS

SCOUT

www.focusreaders.com

Focus Readers is distributed by North Star Editions:
sales@northstareditions.com | 888-417-0195

Produced for Focus Readers by Red Line Editorial.

Photographs ©: Hispanolistic/iStockphoto, cover, 1; ugurhan/iStockphoto, 4 (top); wundervisuals/iStockphoto, 4 (bottom); Monkey Business Images/Shutterstock Images, 7 (top); FrameStockFootages/Shutterstock Images, 7 (bottom), 16 (top right); RgStudio/iStockphoto, 9; Angelo Giampiccolo/Shutterstock Images, 11 (top), 11 (bottom); Ruben M Ramos/Shutterstock Images, 13, 16 (bottom left); CraigRJD/iStockphoto, 15; sumroeng chinnapan/Shutterstock Images, 16 (top left); Artem Oleshko/Shutterstock Images, 16 (bottom right)

Library of Congress Cataloging-in-Publication Data
Library of Congress Cataloging-in-Publication Data is available on the Library of Congress website.

ISBN
978-1-64493-017-5 (hardcover)
978-1-64493-096-0 (paperback)
978-1-64493-254-4 (ebook pdf)
978-1-64493-175-2 (hosted ebook)

Printed in the United States of America
Mankato, MN
012020

About the Author

Connor Stratton enjoys flying to new places, eating popcorn, and watching movies with friends. He lives in Minnesota.

Table of Contents

AIRPORT
ticket agent
ticket

At the Airport

Many people work
at the airport.
Ticket agents work
at the airport.
They give us our **tickets**.

Security officers work
at the airport.
They look at a **screen**.
They look inside our **bags**.

security officer

screen

Airport Helpers

Mechanics work
at the airport.
They fix planes.

mechanic

Controllers work
at the airport.
They look at a screen.
They keep track of planes.
They keep planes safe.

controller

On the Plane

Flight attendants work on the plane. They help us. They give us **drinks**.

flight attendant
drinks

Pilots work on the plane.

They fly the plane.

pilot

Glossary

bags

screen

drinks

tickets

Index